Powerful Strategies 10

Dominate
Binary Options

Jordon Sykes

1

Table Of Contents

Introduction 3

Chapter 1: Technical Analysis Strategy...................................5

Chapter 2: Types Of Binary Options Strategies That Exist ... 8

Chapter 3: Binary Options Basic Strategy 13

Chapter 4: Advanced Binary Options Strategies 28

Chapter 5: Short Term Binary Options Strategy 31

Chapter 6: Long Term Binary Options Strategy................... 41

Chapter 7: Short Term Vs Long Term Binary Strategy 44

Conclusion.. 51

Introduction

Binary Options Strategy

A binary options trading is a widely recognized type of investment where traders can gain more money when they use some strategies effectively or otherwise lose more money if not. Unlike other investment options, this option enables the trader to know how to lose money or to gain. Thus, it involves a known risk. Many traders are making a lot of money from binary options when they make use of effective strategies.

A binary options trading strategy can help one to succeed in this type of investment. In addition, there are expert traders that give tips on how to succeed. These tips can be found at many sites on the internet.There are apparently many strategies on the market that the traders can choose.

The key to the success depends on the effectiveness of the strategy chosen. You should, therefore, devote your time in choosing the best working strategy prior to commencing with your trading. Once you chose the best strategy that you deem effective and successful, you can dedicate time to learning how to it works and how to use it.

Following a strategy when trading digital options may significantly increase your chances to be profitable. However, you should stay realistic and be aware than you can never be certain of success.

Are binary options strategies infallible?

There is no perfect strategy in trading, no matter what any so called "Guru" or signal provider will tell you. All strategies have some flaws and weak points, and there is no such thing as a perfect mathematical model to achieve profits on the financial markets.

When deciding to use a strategy you must be aware all the time that even the best strategy is no guarantee for success. However, this should not discourage you, because certain strategies can be very profitable most of thetimes. You only have to keep in mind that luck is a very important factor in trading, just as it is in life in general.

There are two main strategies used by experts to excel in trading binary options. Newbies also can use these tips and tricks to succeed. Basically, they only need to predict the financial market and then use a winning binary options trading strategy to be really successful. There are many people who have earned more money using strategies and tips, and without these strategies, trading binary options may seem to be a difficult type of investment.

Apparently, there are plenty of strategies on the market with many similarities, but they stem from two main strategies, viz. Fundamental analysis and technical (graphic) analysis. They are explained below:

Chapter 1: Technical Analysis Strategy

This strategy helps one to evaluate the market by using charts to predict the asset prices in the future. The strategy is based on the theory that what has occurred in the past is likely to repeat itself in the future. Traders are predicting the exchange rates using this strategy. Indicators are used to study these charts and detect the patterns that occur.

For this purpose, technical analysis focuses on market movements exclusively. By analyzing past market movements, technical analysts try to understand which psychological dynamics influenced the market in the past and how these dynamics will play out in the future.

This approach sounds more complicated than it is. In our daily lives, we all perform technical analysis. When we meet a new person and they greet us with a bright smile, we predict the possibility of a great new relationship. When they barely notice us, however, we predict that we will never be friends.

Depending on what happens next, we might adjust our prognosis, and we might want to collect more data before decide on our final verdict, but we would try to understand why this person does what it does and then try to predict which actions these motivations create in the future.

Technical analysis does the same thing with an asset's price. If people were willing to buy or sell this asset for certain prices, technical analysis can predict whether these influences will make the price of the asset rise, fall, or move sideways.

Just like in our daily lives, technical analysis defines certain patterns that allow you to predict what will happen next. In our daily lives, we predict that a big smile will lead to friendly interactions; and technical analysis uses similar patterns. There are candlestick formations, trends, technical indicators, and much more. Each of them can help you to predict what will happen next in one glance.

Fundamental Analysis

This is another simple binary options trading strategy without using complicated tools or indicators. This strategy is based on using fundamental economic conditions to predict the direction of market movement. All it takes is to read a lot and be aware of things happening in the global economy.

Let's understand this by a simple example of the global economic happenings in the year 2008 related to banks and other financial institutions regarding loans etc. Though this bubble had been forming since the year 2006, the burst came in 2008 and there was a great hue and cry around the world. Now as a normal smart person it is easy to predict that the circumstances will definitely push the markets down and you should either lessen your investments or buy put in order to gain from the negative market conditions.

Another situation that can be studied to strengthen your faith in this simple binary options trading strategy is that if there is an imminent possibility of a war being declared between 2 countries then it is obvious that the chances of the markets going up are limited while those of the market going down are plenty. There are many such fundamental things which can be used to predict the market movement direction.

The basic awareness that you have about the economy, not just in your country or region but across the globe and the ability to read these signals correctly will decide whether this simple binary options trading strategy works for you or not.

This strategy works most of the time but always remember-nothing is right 100% of the time. Gradually as you gain experience it will become easier for you to be able to predict correctly. This strategy focuses on economic indicators to predict the market. These economic indicators help to predict the exchange rate, and they are obtained by analyzing the historical data of the market.

From this data, traders observe the data to predict the price range of certain assets, and they also consider factors that influenced the price range. These factors could be employment statistics, political influences, or other critical information.

For newcomers, a news-based approach is the most intuitive strategy. With this strategy, you would invest in rising prices whenever positive news about an asset reaches the market, and you would invest in falling prices whenever negative news about an asset reaches the market.

To help you execute such a strategy effectively, most brokers offer economic calendars on their websites. Whenever important news is about to be published, for example, unemployment data or a company's earnings report, these calendars will tell you what the market expects, which helps you to decide which news would be good and which would be bad, and in which direction you should invest.

Trading the news is simple, intuitive, and easy-to-learn, but it also has disadvantages. When news reaches the market, it often reacts in unpredictable ways. Additionally, even if positive news makes the market rise, it is often difficult to predict how far it will rise and for how long. While news traders accept these uncertainties and claim that they can make a profit anyway, traders have developed technical analysis to be able to predict market movements independently from all outer influences.

Chapter 2: Types Of Binary Options Strategies That Exist

Generally speaking, there are two main categories of strategies when it comes to binary trading:

Type 1: Strategies based on betting models - Those strategies presume that using specific patterns in terms of investment amounts and the right timing can generate profit no matter if the trader is skilled or not at market prediction. Those strategies presume that in certain situations you can design your option buying strategy to give you a high probability of winning. In this category, you will find betting pattern strategies like The Grinding Strategy or strategies based on trading the news.

Type 2: Strategies on how to predict the direction of the market better - In this case the strategies are based on simple technical and statistical evidence that in some circumstances the market has greater chances to move in one direction over another. While technical analysis can be pretty complicated, there are much simpler ways of interpreting the charts, especially when it comes to binary trading.

The strategy that we are going to present is a very simple "Type 2" strategy. It's purpose is to help you predict the direction of the market movement and have a high percentage of options that finish in the money. This strategy is based on the assumption that markets tend to correct themselves after movements in one direction, and the price usually goes up and down. This means that if the price has raised in the previous timeframe, it is more likely to fall in the next one.

Of course, this is not a rule and there will be many times when it won't happen, especially when the market is on a trend, but when the market is calm and fluctuations are at small levels (a low volatility) you will most likely see ups and downs constantly.

Binary options usually have a small timeframe and are ideal for this type of technique. The trading platforms of the brokers will show you a recent chart of the asset that is well suited for the option's timeframe. If an option expires in 15

minutes, you are likely to see the chart for the last 45 minutes and an empty chart for the next 15 minutes like in Figure 1:

Figure 1: USD/JPY one hour binary option chart

If the current price is higher than the opening price (in the current sample the current price of 79.7199 is higher than the opening price of 79.6921) the price is more likely to move down, and you should buy a PUT option. In the opposite situation, when the current price is lower than the opening price you should buy a CALL option as the market is expected to move up.

After buying the PUT option you must wait until the expiry time, which is 15 minutes in this case. Let's see how the chart looked like after 15 minutes:

The price moved down to 79.7032 and the option finished "in the money" generating a profit of 81% in only 15 minutes. As you can see, the price followed the tendency to normalize after a small increase and finished closer to the opening value. While this outcome is more likely to happen than the opposite, you should expect a decent amount of trades to end up the wrong way.

Figure 2: USD/JPY chart after option expiry

You should also keep in mind when using this strategy that sometime the market is on a trend or some important news may be released that will shake the market to a degree that such simplistic analysis will be useless. This strategy is recommended on calm markets with small trading volumes and no news expected to be released in the following hours.

In order to have good performance while trading binary options it is advisable to have a strategy. Relying on luck is not a good option since it will turn your investment into gambling, and eventually you will end up losing. There are two important aspects when talking about binary options trading:

- Having some good technique to help you predict the market correctly in most of the situations

- Having a good strategy regarding the use of binary options in a way that greatly increases your winning chances

While predicting the market correctly is very good and can make you a profitable trader in almost any circumstances, there are certain strategies that can generate very good profits even for traders who are not very skilled at identifying market trends.

General Tips For Improving Results

Here are some basic tips that will help you identify the direction where the market is heading:

- Watch the charts for longer periods of time, and identify the current market trend. It is well known among professional traders that trading against the trend is not recommended unless you know very well what you're doing

- Big spikes in the charts mean that the asset was bought or sold in large quantities in a very small period of time. This happens mostly because speculative investors are trying to obtain short-term profits. In order for them to be in profit they must close their positions, which mean they must sell what they initially bought, or vice-versa. This phenomenon is called "marking the profit" and has an opposite impact on the market than the initial movement. That means that every time you will see a big spike in the charts, it is very likely to see normalization afterwards. If the market raised excessively it is time to sell.

- Watch an economic calendar in order to know what to expect. At certain announcements the market becomes very volatile, and you must adapt your trading strategies accordingly.

- If you are more experienced in trading you can use technical indicators in order to identify trends and market movements. This is recommended only for advanced traders who know what they are doing. Technical indicators can be very tricky if they are used wrongly, and we advise you to stay away from them unless you understand the phenomenon very well. There are plenty of other ways to make profits trading with binary options, so this is not a big inconvenient. However, if you are skilled with technical analysis you should take advantage of it because it can be a very potent tool combined with the advantages of binary trading.

Another great way of improving results in binary trading is by using signals from experienced traders. While finding a good singal providing service can be pretty hard and expensive, sometimes there are also affordable options that may prove to deliver a very good return on investment.

Some people prefer to use automatic systems for trading (also known as algorithmic trading) and let the computer trade by itself. This hands free approach has the advantage of not requiring much effort and time, but those using it must always check the performance and adjust their strategies to maximize the results. When it comes to binary options you can check the algorithmic trading service from Option Bit namedAlgobit.

Chapter 3: Binary Options Basic Strategy

The basic strategy is a simple but effective strategy for binary traders. This strategy can be used when the trades start in the correct direction. That means that if you bought a call option and the market raised (you are in the money but still need to wait until the expiry) you can use this strategy to aim high with low risks. The strategy is best described with an example, so this is what we'll do. Here is a sample on how this strategy can be used:

Step 1: You buy a call option on EUR/USD at 1.3500 worth $100 with the expiry in one hour, a payout of 80% and a refund of 10%.

The market moves in your favor to 1.3520 (20 points in the first 15 minutes). In this given situation, the strategy can be used as described in the next step.

Step 2: You buy a put option on the same asset (EUR/USD in this case) with the same value at 1.3520 (the option must have the same expiry as the initial one, and it will have the same payouts since it is on the same asset).

There are three possibilities at the expiry:

1) The closing price is above 1.3520 -> the first option finishes in the money and the second one out of the money. Total investment $200 and total payout $190 ($180 from the winning option and a $10 refund from the losing one). Outcome: a loss of only $10

2) The closing price is between 1.3500 and 1.3520 -> both options finish in the money. Total investment is still $200 and total payout is $360. Outcome: a profit of $160

3) The closing price is below 1.3500 -> the first option finishes out of the money while the second one finishes in the money. The outcome is the same as in the first situation: a loss of $10

As you can see from the above example, by using this basic strategy you can take advantage of a good start and risk only an insignificant amount with the chance of winning big. In this particular situation you risk to lose $10 in order to win $160, which is a reward to risk ratio of 16 to 1!

Touch Options Strategy For News Trading (TOSNT)

The TOSNT can be use only when trading the news, as the name suggests, and requires a broker that allows Touch Options. If you are not familiar with news trading, you can't use this strategy. If you know what news trading is and what happens with the markets during the news, this strategy may be your lucky bullet to success. As with all the strategies presented here, we will use an example in order to make it easier for you to follow.

Step 1: You are ready for the release of big news that will shake the markets. The NFP (Non-farm Payrolls) is a good example of such news that affects the US Dollar. 10 minutes before the news is released you take action.

Step 2: You buy a Touch Up Option and a Touch Down Option with the same value, at the same time. Let's say you are trading on EUR/USD and the price is 1.3500. The Touch Up option will pay you 250% profit if the pair will hit the price of 1.3525 in the next 20 minutes. The Touch Down will pay you 250% profit if the pair hits 1.3475 in the next 20 minutes. That means that if the market will move more than 25 points in the next 20 minutes in any direction, one of your touch options will hit.

Since the NFP shakes the market with at least 50 points every time, one of your options will surely hit. If you are lucky enough and the market move both ways before deciding which direction it goes you can even hit both targets. If you hit only one of the touch options (this will happen in most of the cases) and you invested

$100 in each option, you will get a $350 payout for the winning option and zero for the losing one. That means a net profit of $150.

Hitting both options is pretty uncommon, but if you are lucky enough to be in this situation you will make a profit of $500! If you chose the right news that move the markets well enough you are almost certain to win with this strategy. The key to success with this strategy is to choose the right news and have good timing.

The simplicity of Binary Options has enabled the person on the street to get into trading without having to learn the in-depth strategies of conventional trading. As a result, it has brought a lot of new money into the trading scene to the delight of the average on-the-street investor. The simplicity of the Price Up or the Price Down and two mouse click trading with as much as an 81% profit has caught the attention of a whole new segment of investors.

"RTSB" – The Simplified Strategy

Along with the simplified trading comes a simplified strategy for trading Binary Options. I like to call it "RTSB" which stands for "Read the Screen Bud". Yep, that is right. Open your eyes, turn off the TV, stop texting your friends, close your chat room windows, and look at what is on the trading screen right in front of you. In addition to displaying the current price and trading period every Binary Options trading screen has a button that will allow you to display the chart of the previous trading period.

While "RTSB" is the visual cue to look at what is in front of you the analytical cue is for you to look at whether the price of the Asset is going Up or Down. The direction of movement is called the Trend Line and the question you need to answer for yourself is whether the Trend is going Up or is it going Down.If the Trend is going Up then you would consider making a CALL trade. However, if the Trend is going Down you want to consider making a PUT trade.

The "DDSS" Strategy

The "DDSS" Strategy is also quite simple, "Don't Do Something Stupid". This strategy is best explained by an example. As you are looking at the charts for the Asset and you see the current price start to go Up then a few minutes later it goes Down by an almost equal amount, then a few minutes after that it goes Up again. If you look at the average price during this time period you should see that it remains almost the same. Some traders call it "Flatlined", but the trading term is " Sideways Moving". This is where you apply the "DDSS" strategy and DO NOT make any Trades for that Asset. A Sideways Moving price is very hard to predict and most of the time your prediction will be wrong. Stay away from it and look for another Asset that has an obvious Up or Down Trend Line.

I must admit, the RTSB and DDSS strategies are real attention getters to highlight that you must pay attention to what you are doing as you can lose money fast if you do not do your own research before trading.

The Spread Strategy

The Spread Strategy is a real trading strategy that has also been simplified by Binary Options trading. In conventional options trading, you use the Spread or Straddle strategy to buy CALLS and sell PUTS on the same Asset. However, in Binary Options trading you can't place a Call and PUT trade for the same Asset unless you are using two different trading Brokers which is not recommended.

The basic idea of the Spread in Binary Options is to find two Assets where the Trend line is Up for one and Down for the other. On the Asset that the Trend line is up you place a CALL trade on it while on the Asset where the Trend line is down you place a PUT trade on it at the same time.

The Spread strategy is often called "hedging your bet". If both trades end In-the-Money you could receive an 81% payout on both of them. A $100 Trade Price on each of the trades would result in a $162 profit. However, if one trade ends Out-of-the-Money you have minimized your loss to $19; $100 loss on one trade and $81 profit on the other trade. However, if both trades are Out-of-the-Money you would have a $162 loss.

Hedging Strategies

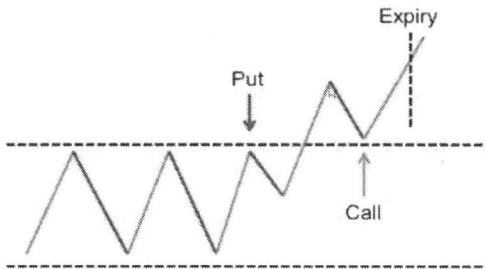

Hedging is a strategy that is used by individual operators to reduce investment risk through various methods such as buying and selling options, marketing techniques or futures contracts in the short term. The hedging strategies are designed to reduce volatility and potential risk of a portfolio or an investment to reduce the risk of loss. Basically, there is the advantage of blocking existing benefits. Hedging strategies are used most frequently, while Forex Trading and binary options are also used along with hedging strategies to minimize the risk of loss.

This strategy is commonly known as Pairing and most often used along with corporations in binary options traders, investors and traditional stock-exchanges, as a means of protection and to minimize the associated risks. This strategy is executed by placing both Call and Puts on the same asset at the same time. This assures that regardless of the direction of the asset value, the trade will generate a successful outcome. This provides the investor with profits of an "in the money" outcome. This is a great means of protecting yourself as an investor in whichever scenario is produced. It's sort of an insurance method that prepares you for any scenario.

For some time now, binary options trading have been used for daily transactions. Although it may sound strange, but a merchant who has a thorough knowledge of binary options can be used for partial coverage. It also gives an opportunity to reap more profits. The rational use of call and put options can reduce risks further. In fact, profits can be double-binary options if executed properly.

binary options hedging strategy is to understand hedging. Hedging basically means controlling or mitigating risks. For example, insurance is a hedge against unforeseen calamity or disaster. In case of trading, a typical example of hedging would be going long on a financial asset and going short on an opposite or competing asset. The idea is that both these assets cannot move in the same direction, upward or downward, at a given period of time.

Therefore, there would be profit from one and loss from other, resulting in a moderate gain or as less a loss as possible. Hedging is popularly used in volatile market conditions to maximize gains and minimise loss.

How Hedging Strategy Works?

One of the popular binary options hedging strategy is known as the straddle. A straddle is difficult to execute because it requires identifying the highest and the lowest levels of an asset price during a trading period. There would be two binary options involved in this case- a call option on the highest level and a put option on the lowest level. An ideal period for this kind of binary options hedging strategy is when the price is moving symmetrically. A trader, might also want to bet on two positions in the same direction, instead of opposing directions, in case the there is strong trending price movement.

Binary options hedging strategy may also involve currency pairs. In fact, hedging as an advanced risk mitigation financial strategy initially was developed for trading in foreign currencies. For this kind of hedging strategy, a trader needs to find out a pair of currencies that usually move in opposite directions. Two binary options, each on each of the currencies will mean profit from either of the two in a given period, as price of one will go up while the other goes down.

Binary options hedging strategy might also involve one touch binary options. The inherent risks of a one touch or touch/no touch binary options are very high. But, at the same time one can gain even up to a 600% profit. This kind of strategy can be used when the market is strongly trending.

Buying two binary options in this case will involve two trigger values of the same financial asset's price. In the best case scenario, there could be profit from both positions. But in the worst case there would be bigger loss. The third, moderate possibility is one loss and one win.

While formulating a binary options hedging strategy, a trader may want to buy both binary options to be expired in the same period or different periods. For example one may predict, based on the market dynamics and indicators that the market might go up in the next few days or week, but come down after, say, a month. So, the two binary options, the trader buys may expire in two different periods.

Whatever type of binary options hedging strategy one chooses to adapt, it is crucial to observe the market movement closely before betting. Although trading or hedging in binary options is more like betting, it should not be based on pure gut feeling. The decision should have some sound reason behind it. And, no matter what, one should always look for opportunities to hedge the risk.

As a trader, know that the majority of binary options trades concluded at the end of the day or every hour. If the price of a particular action, i.e. $ 20 and can make a profit of $ 200, now if prices rise as his prediction in an hour before it expires, you have the option of whether to hold or sell the quota before the expiration. The decision to retain the fee depends on many factors. The future depends on market and other sources of information that helps traders analyze the market.

Now, in this particular case, you can use partial or full coverage. Full coverage involves the sale of all shares in this scenario. This would bring benefits in the given time. Partial coverage means to retain some shares, while selling some of them. Although there is some risk attached as trade, to some extent still is open, but risk losing the shares sold is reduced. If at the time of expiration, the trader's prediction is correct, would have the benefit, but without involving any risk.

When To Use Hedging Strategy?

However, if you are heading strategies using the binary option, there are many things, which you have to consider. Below listed are some of these things:

Identifying the risks: The decision to hedge or not depends mainly on the risks that the company is exposed. These risks are financial and operational risks. In general, operating risks cannot be covered, and which are not traded. Hand on financial risks can be covered, as are traded on the market.

Differentiate between speculation and coverage: The managers must distinguish between coverage and speculation. Provided adequate coverage reduces risk and not to be confused with speculation.

Compare the cost of coverage: Sometimes the cost of coverage forces manager's non-coverage. However, sometimes the cost of coverage will be inexpensive as the potential losses faced by the company due to the market factors. Therefore, proper evaluation is a necessity

Understand the tools of the coverage: It is important to understand the hedging instruments for the right application. The lack of this knowledge can lead to managers not to cover.

Using a hedging strategy enables a trader to execute two options closely together in order to maximize his profits with a lower level of risk. For instance, if you successfully traded a call option on JPMorgan Chase & Co but believe it will fall in the next hour; you can implement a hedging strategy by pairing a put option on JPMorgan Chase & Co stock alongside a call option on the asset. This will allow you to hedge against both eventualities and safeguard your initial return

However, a carefully designed hedging strategy reduces costs and risks. An option to carry out this strategy is very simple, as it is easy to understand and manage. Proper use of strategies for binary options on the coverage of this kind can help merchants protect themselves and maximize their profit.

Trend Trading Strategy

A basic strategy most adopted by beginners as well as experienced traders. This strategy is often referred to as the bull-bear strategy and focuses on monitoring, rising, declining and the flat trend line of the traded asset. If there is a flat trend line and a prediction that the asset price will go up, the No Touch Option is recommended.

If the trend line shows that the asset is going to rise, choose CALL.

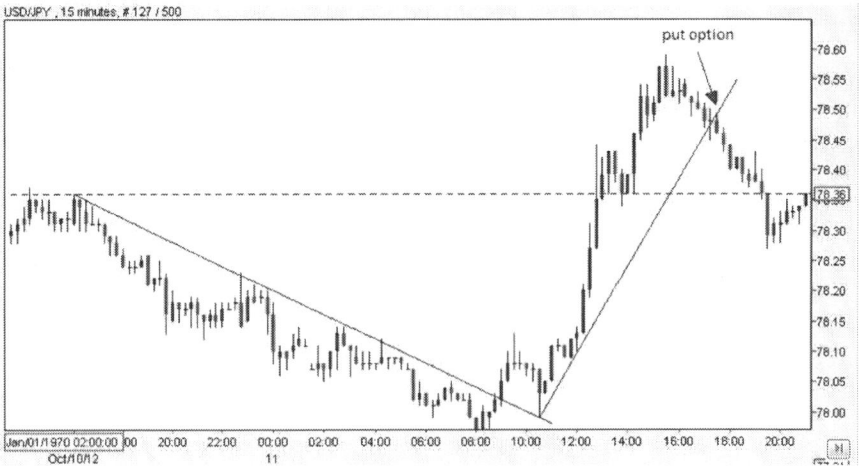

If the trend line shows a decline in the price of the asset, choose PUT.

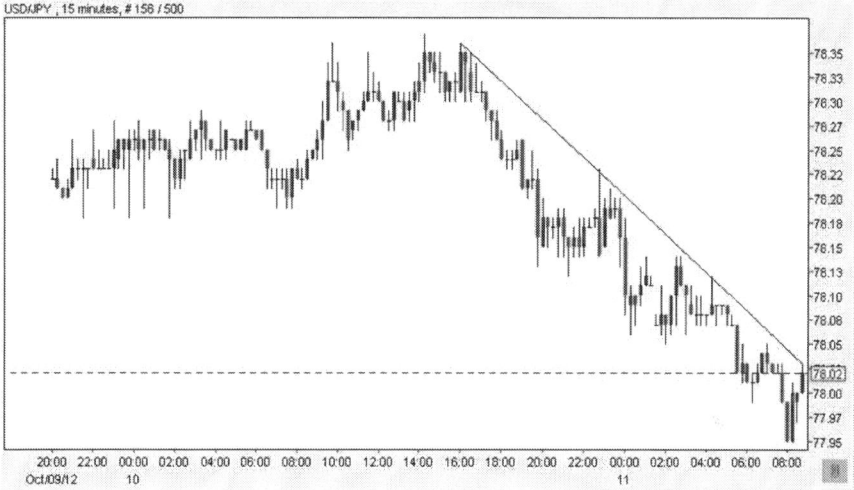

USD/JPY , 15 minutes, # 156 / 500

This method works the same as the CALL/PUT option except in this case, you select the price at which the asset must not reach before the selected period. For example, Google's share price is $540 and the trading platform is on the No Touch price of $570 with percentage returns of 77%. If the price doesn't reach $570 after the specified time, then there is a gain.

Most financial speculators who utilize binary options have followed so called trend trading strategies with binary options as methods for optimizing their returns. Trend trading binary options refer to watching the gains and losses of the chosen market, and figuring out the chances for the momentum to continue or reverse. It still relies on on the original binary format, but adds the wisdom of market flow concepts from careful monitoring and applying basic principles.

Fiscally defined, the word 'trend' pertains to the overriding path that the value of a plus point travels, which is either over one or more time sections. Lesser term trends subsist as elements of more substantial trends that last for various lengths of time. It is imperative to recognize the movement over the interval and comprehend the bigger picture before deciding to buy and sell.

The popularity of trading trends is attributable mostly to the ease of setting bets, as well as the comparatively small outlay and quick as well as high turnarounds, which are possible. Added to that, casual traders and hopeful investors are showing more interest in opportunism afforded by current economic markets. Some platforms are reporting earnings from trend trading binary options in excess of 82 percent of the time, consistently.

Since trend trading with digital options is not a finite system, the kind of wisdom it takes to collect consistently massive profits is not something that can be taught without incorporating experience. It behooves investors, for this reason, to learn to restrain their immediate sentiments and instead keep calm before selecting their next move. Reactionary bets throw trend trading triumphs to the wind.

Most authorities in Forex, as well as those in digital options trading, advise avoiding the elephant approach that has the investor dumping heavily in one place. Diversifying funds is just as important in binary options trend trading as it is anywhere else. That, and reserving your bets to right money, or disposable funding.

Pinocchio Strategy

This strategy is utilized when the asset price is expected to rise or fall drastically in the opposite direction. If the value is expected to go up, select CALL and if it's expected to drop, select PUT. This is best practiced on a free demo account from one of the brokers.

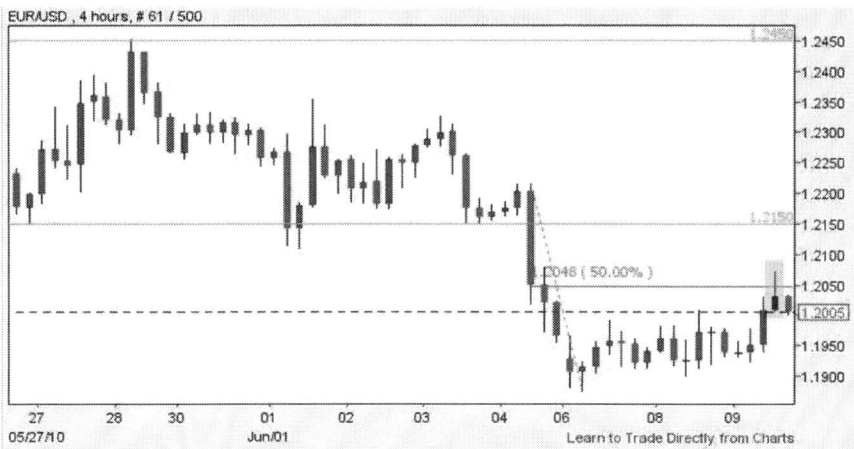

EUR/USD , 4 hours, # 61 / 500

Learn to Trade Directly from Charts

Straddle Strategy

This strategy is best applied during market volatility and just before the break of important news related to specific stock or when predictions of analysts seem to be afloat. This is a highly regarded strategy utilized throughout the global community of trading. This is a strategy best known for presenting an ability to the trader to avoid the CALL and PUT option selection, but instead putting both on a selected asset.

The overall idea is to utilize PUT when the value of the asset is increased, but there is an indication or belief that it will being to drop soon. Once the decline sets in, place the CALL option on it, expecting it to actually bounce back soon. This can also be done in the reverse direction, by placing CALL on a those assets priced low and PUT on the rising asset value. This greatly increases chances of success in at least one of the trade options by producing an "in the money" result. The straddle strategy is greatly admired by traders when the market is up and down or when a particular asset has a volatile value.

The straddle strategy is more appropriate for daily options as it gives the asset a slightly longer timeframe to react to changes in

25

the market. With this strategy, you would also place a call and a put option on an asset. However, you will also need to watch the movements of the asset very closely in order to ensure you know when to place the call or put option on the asset during the day

Risk Reversal Strategy

This is indeed one of the most highly regarded strategies among experienced binary options traders across the globe. It aims to lower the risk factor associated with trading and increase the chances of a successful outcome that results in positive profit gains. This strategy is executed by placing CALL and PUT options simultaneously on an individual underlying asset. This is especially beneficial when trading on assets with fluctuating values. Naturally, binary options can experience two possible outcomes and trading on a two for two opposite's predictions over an individual asset at once, guarantees that at least one will generate a positive outcome.

Using this strategy can be effective when trading on hourly options. If an asset is trending in a particular direction that isn't typical for the asset, you can place a trade on the asset which highlights that it is likely change course in a short space of time

Market Volatility Test Strategy

This simple binary option trading strategy is based on the volatility of markets, so all you need to understand before placing your trade is to know whether the asset on which you are trading is going up or down.

The simple basis of this strategy is that the market corrects itself after a certain period of time and studying the movement of the asset that you want to trade in and predict whether the asset will move up or down in the next 15 minutes. This is a simple binary options trading strategy where once you enter your broker's trading platform with the 15 minute trading option you are going to see a chart showing the movement of the asset over the last 45 minutes.

When you see the chart, you have to see the direction against the opening price. If the current value of the asset is lower than its opening price then you should buy a call option based on this theory of market correction according to which the market corrects itself.

So as the price had been going down, now it should go up. On the other hand if the current price is more than the original price, you should buy a put as the price is likely to fall. The average of this strategy being successful is about 60%; but don't think that this is a bad average because whenever you are successful you may make upto 85% of the original amount

Chapter 4: Advanced Binary Options Strategies

Advanced strategy: binary options combined with classical trading

The Advanced Strategy for Binary Options and Classical Trading (ASBOCT) is another strategy developed by our team's strategist. Just like the TOSNT described above, this strategy cannot be reproduced on other websites, and those who wish to use it are free to do it while taking full responsibility for their actions. We don't guarantee results and cannot be held liable if using our strategies results in loses for you. As a trader you decide if you want to use the strategies found here at your own risk.

The ASBOCT is an advanced strategy because it requires you to use a binary options broker that offers Touch Options and a classical forex broker (or CFD broker if you want to use it for commodities, indices or stocks). We recommend using 24 Option or Option Fair for the touch options and any of the following brokers for the classical trading: Markets.com, Ava Trade or XM. This strategy is very difficult to use for US traders because they will have a hard time finding a good forex broker, but if you are from US and already trade with a forex broker, you can use it as well.

To understand this strategy you must have good knowledge of traditional forex trading. If you don't know the basics of traditional trading then this strategy is not for you.

This strategy is pretty similar to the TOSNT in the way that it is best used when market moves are expected. It can be used before news releases or in very volatile market conditions. If your technical analysis detects a possible burst in one direction of the market, but you don't know in which direction, this is another good moment to use this strategy.

The Grinding Strategy

The grinding strategy is a simple yet effective strategy that is based on the fact that the market cannot move in the same direction in too many consecutive periods. As you know, the market goes up and down, and this is why this strategy is very effective on binary options.

Using this strategy, you will start from an initial investment amount and increase it every time your option expires out of the money. You will continue to buy the same option on the same asset one after another, at a higher value. This way, you are certain to win after maximum 3 to 5 options, and because of the value increase you will recover all previous losses and generate profit as well.

Here is an example, of how this strategy works. You buy a Call option on Gold with the payout of 85% and no refund. You invest $100 in this option. If you win you get a profit of $85 and immediately purchase a Put option on the same asset (gold in this case), right after the expiry. If the market goes down and you win again, you buy a Call option. If the market goes up and down all the time you win $85 at every cycle.

If the market moves against you when you bought a Call option and you lose, you immediately buy another Call option worth $250 (2.5 times the initial value, if your initial option has a different value). If you win, you will get $212 profit that will compensate for the initial $100 loss and still give you a $112 total profit. After your win, you start again with the value of $100 in the opposite direction.

In the unlucky event where you have two losses in a row, you continue in the same direction with a value worth 2 times the previous one ($500 if your initial option was $100). If the option is a winner, you will get $425 in profit that will cover for the initial losses of $100 and $250 generating an overall profit of $75. After every win, you start again on the opposite direction with the initial value.

Since markets cannot move in the same direction too many times in a row, you are sure to win with a few tries. This is why this strategy it is called grinding: because every time you win an amount proportional to your initial investment. Whenever you lose, you increase the bet amount by 2.5 or by 2, depending on the sequence.

As you can see this strategy cannot fail. The only thing you should worry about is your total capital, that must be large enough compared to the initial investment in order to be able to cover a few consecutive losses. Other things you should consider when using this strategy is the maximum value allowed by the broker, and the time the market stops. Make sure you have at least 8 sequences before the market takes a break. If you trade using 30 minutes options, you should make sure there are at least 4 hours of trading ahead.

Chapter 5: Short Term Binary Options Strategy

Short Term Binary Options Strategy (contracts) come in many flavors; the most popular of them being the 30 second, 1 minutes or 5 minutes and 15 minutes expiries. (read more about Expiry Times) This short term expiry contracts is traded the most due to the fast paced action that they offer. Short term binary options typically payout between 65% – 80% and is mostly available for forex instruments. In this article, you will learn about a few simple strategies that you can use to trade these short-term binary options expiring contracts.

30 Seconds Binary Options Strategy

In 30 seconds binary options strategy, the time to make a decision is very less (30 seconds). So it is very important to make the right decision to ensure return on the investment made. After choosing the right charting system and analyzing the market trend, the trader should understand the terms- call and put.

If the market is green and on the rising trend, probability is that the asset price would also be increasing & the trader would see green bars on the chart. If the trader feels that the asset price would increase over the 30 second interval, he can buy a call which means that the price of the asset at the expiry would be more than the current price at the expiry time of the 30 seconds binary option strategy.

If on the other hand, the market is on a downward trend and the price of the asset is decreasing, the trader can buy a put which means that the price of the asset at the expiry time would be less than the current price.

Depending upon the decision and the status of the asset in the 30 seconds binary option strategy, the trader can either expect a return or loss of the entire investment. If the judgment and decision is correct, the trader would receive a fixed return irrespective of the price of the asset. However on the contrary, the trader loses all the investment if the trader wages incorrectly.

How To Trade 30 Seconds Strategy?

There are some important steps involved in the 30 seconds binary options strategy. The first step involves the market study. It is very important to study the market in order to decide the financial asset. The choice of financial asset depends upon a lot of factors like investment amount, asset category amongst other stocks in the market, the performance of the asset over a quarter, predictions of the result of the asset in the next quarter and so on. Thus it is very important to do a good amount of research before deciding upon the asset.

The next step in 30 seconds binary options strategy involves selecting the charting system for which the trader can contact his broker or can search one online. The chart system should also have open-high-low-close bars to give a pictorial representation of the fluctuation in the price of the asset. The fluctuations are depicted in an interval of 30 seconds. The green bars would represent increase in the price of the asset and red bars would represent the decreasing pattern of the asset. The trader should wait and analyze the pattern for minimum 3 bars in order to understand the trend of the market and trend of the asset.

The market trend is not constant and every second counts, so it is very important for the trader to stay focused. The 30 seconds binary option strategy is even more tempting as compared to 5 mins as it gives an option to earn good return in short duration of time. At the same time, it also increases the chances of losing the investment if the decision is not accurate. At the end of the day it's all about money and how the trader plays with it.

One Touch Binary Options Strategy

One touch binary option, among these, is an exotic variety that can last for a week or hour or minutes, and gets automatically executed. It is one directional in nature.

"One directional" implies that a trader starts with a price of an underlying financial asset, and bets whether that price will touch a predetermined level, say within a week. This predetermined level of price is known as the trigger value. If at any time during the trading week, the price reaches that level, the option gets executed and the trader receives the profit. With a solid one touch binary options strategy, a trader can make more than 100% profit.

In fact, these options are usually the ones that provide the highest payoffs. This particular characteristic, where the trader does not have to wait till the expiration of the option to exercise it, makes one touch options an American style of options. If, on the other hand, the price does not reach this predetermined level, there is no earning at all. This is why one touch binary option strategy is gaining so much in popularity nowadays.

How One Touch Strategy Works?

To understand how one makes profit in one touch binary options, one must understand that although it is related to the price of the underlying asset, the difference between this price and investment is not the profit. A trader can invest a particular amount in the betting process. Depending on the trading platform, the rate of potential profit may vary. Since these are high risk options, many trading platforms or broker offer profit rates like 400% or more or less.

So, if a trader has invested a $100, with a profit rate of 400% he may earn a total of $500 in case the betting is a success. For example, if at the time of buying the option the trader betted on the price of an asset to increase from $X to $Y within a week's time period. If the price does increase to $Y in that week, he will make a 400% profit on his investment, in this case $100. This profit percentage is not calculated on the price of the asset. Therefore, one stop binary options strategy will involve predicting this price movement reliably and correctly. The following section discusses what are required to develop such a strategy.

How To Trade One Touch Strategy?

Trading of one touch binary options strategy depends on conditions of the market, the asset, and volatility of the same. Many new traders have this misconception that in case of one touch options, one bets on whether the price will change or not. But it is not the case. A trader here bets on whether the price will change to a particular level within a given time frame.

One touch binary options strategy is primarily based on market movements. This means that if the prices of commodities, stocks, foreign currencies or indexes are being stable for a while, then betting on price movement is not logical. When the prices are volatile, it is more ideal situation for trading in one touch binary options.

Like any other binary options, it is important to understand in case of one touch options that there is never a guaranteed success. Therefore, success of one touch binary options strategy may come after a while. Partly, this success depends on on trader's professional discipline.

It is absolutely critical to follow financial news on a daily basis. With that information a trader may be able to predict market movement with greater reliability. Since, one touch options are not high/low or rise/fall; instead touching or not touching a particular value, one touch binary options strategy will require the trader to predict price of the underlying financial asset for a short duration. Because of this, trader must also develop knowledge and insights regarding individual assets, on which he is betting. Another critical aspect, on which the trader must develop reliable expertise, is predicting price volatility, which can be developed over time.

5 Minutes Binary Options Strategy

The 5 minute Binary Option Strategy is a good way to begin trading in binary options and investing online. This way you can learn about the basic technical indicators used along with making some profit for yourself, thus making it a good introductory strategy.

The 5 minute Binary options strategy helps the trader to make the maximum number of transactions per a single session as the analysis are done by him are on a 1-minute chart and then their execution is done further in 5 minutes.

The basic strategy that is used is to look out for those points of resistance that expect only short term reversals for making an entry. Once the basics of trading are clear, the strategy used can be modified to deal in larger time frames.

In order to achieve the maximum benefits from the 5 minute binary options strategy, a trader needs to figure out the most suitable platform for the 5 minute binary options strategy. There are many platforms and binary options trading systems that can be utilized. Those automated trading tools are available for free on the internet and can be used, so it's very important to invest a good amount of time in researching the most safe and profitable binary option software before investing funds in the stocks.

How 5 Minutes Binary Options Strategy Works?

There are two basic requirements for the 5 minute binary options strategy to work:

• Chart: Displays the movement of stock prices and your trade.

• Oscillator: The oscillator works in accordance to the chart and shows the visual representation of the progress – ups and downs – of a particular stock right from the starting of the first minute till the end of the fifth. We have to use five minutes time frame since it is the 5 minute binary options strategy.

3 Steps for The 5 Minutes Binary Options Strategy

This is how 5 Minutes binary options strategy works. It requires the completion of only 3 easy steps. Let's take a look at how they go:

• Step 1: The first step in the 5 minute binary options strategy involves choosing the asset you would like to trade.

• Step 2: Once you have decided on the asset, you would need to go online and select a charting system.

Step 3: It involves using open-high-low-close bars in your 5 minute chart. Each line on the chart would cover a period of 5 minutes depicting the price range of your asset in 5 minutes. After 5 minutes, a bar would show if the price of the asset is increasing or decreasing over a period of 5 minutes.

This 5 Minute Binary Options Strategy is quite simple and requires you to focus on one trading indicator or currency pair. The next task should be to find the Derivative Oscillator indicator. This indicator is easily observed with some discipline and focus. You would notice a trend-generating and trend-scouting indicator that could be applied directly to the price movement direction of our targeted asset.

On average, traders' profitability and success rates are confirmed to be about 73%. This is only when applying the said technique.

Short Term Binary Option Expiries

The short term binary options expiries are contracts that expire within a short period of time. A trader is paid out a fixed return if the contract expires in-the-money or loses their risked investment if it expires out-of-the-money. On a broader perspective, short term expiries behave the same way as any other long term binary options expiries. The fun and excitement comes from speculating the price moves over a short period of time. Technical analysts in forex often argue that it is a lot easier to predict where price moves in the short term than in the long term. But do not be fooled. It is very easy to get addicted to trading the short term expiries and a trader can quickly lose all of their equity when they take consecutive losses.

Trading News Releases with Short Term Binary Options Strategy

Below, we outline a few simple to use trading strategies that can be applied to the short term expiring binary options contracts.

In forex, it is often said to buy the rumor and sell the fact. This simple logic works very well with short term options. The way to trade short term contracts is to first look for a major news release. This could the NFP that is very volatile and affects most of the majors. It could also be central bank interest rate decisions or even CPI data.

The next step is to look for the sentiment. Usually, media starts to report about the estimates on such events 24 – 48 hours ahead of the news. If the general sentiment is bullish, then 5 minutes ahead of the news release, make sure to purchase a CALL option. Choosing the expiry time is of importance here as a small miscalculation can lead to a loss. Typically, choose contracts that expire close to the news release time.

For example, if a CPI news release is due to be out at 10GMT and the market is expecting a bullish reading, then purchase a CALL option 3 – 4 minutes before the news release. Choose either a 60-second expiry or 2 minutes expiring contracts. Price usually tends to rally before the news and then drop back after the news is released.

To compare, a forex trader usually employs such a strategy known as scalping to make some high probability profits before, during and after the news release. (see Economic calendar with news here)

Short Term Binary Options – Trading Example

AUDUSD – Unemployment Release: The chart below shows the 1 minute chart of AUDUSD before the Australia Unemployment data was released. Notice how price spiked just around the time the report was released. A CALL option around 0.9324 with a 2 – 5-minute expiry would have resulted in a winning trade. But notice the importance of timing here. If the option was a 60 second expiry, it would have resulted in a loss.

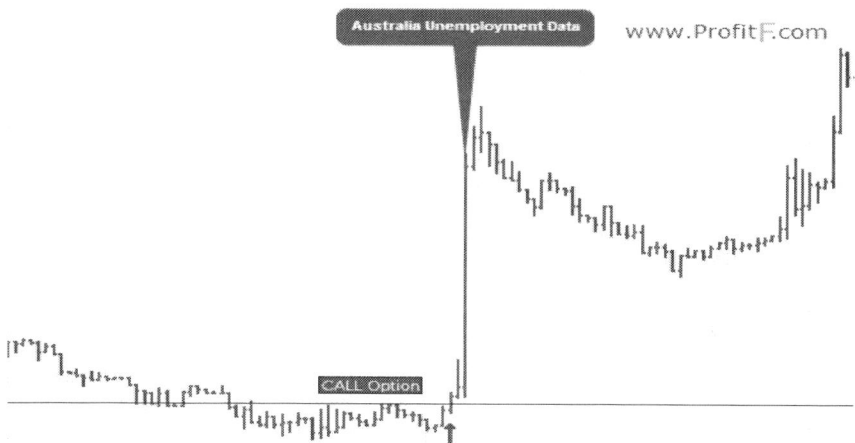

Australia Unemployment Data

www.ProfitF.com

CALL Option

NZDUSD Unemployment Release: The next example below shows the Kiwi unemployment data. Keeping in line with the buy the rumor sells the fact strategy, notice how price spiked ahead of the news release. The unemployment rate had actually increased from 5.8% to 6%, which is not great news. However, despite the actual release, price rallied before the news was released. In this chart, we see that a 2 minute expiry just before the news release would have resulted in a winning trade. Again, in this chart, we would like to stress the importance of timing the trade and choosing the right expiry time.

A minute ahead or later would have resulted in a losing trade due to the fast changing price. After making the spike, price moved within a tight range without any direction and it would have caught many traders who were late to the party... or some greedy traders opening new contracts resulting in a losing trade

CALL Option

Trading Short Term Contracts – Takeaway

From the above examples, we see that while it is simple to trade news releases with short term expiring contracts, traders need to get in on a contract at the right time and price. And don't forget choose regulated Binary Options Broker (see our Top Binary options brokers) A small miscalculation on the timing of the contract expiry or even if the price moved too much before you could enter the contract could jeopardize the chances of having a winning trade.

For traders who are just starting out with trading the short term expiring contracts, always trade with the minimum investment amount for the contract so as to keep your losses to the minimum.

Chapter 6: Long Term Binary Options Strategy

Long-term binary options contracts are something new in the world of binary trading. They appeared sometimes around 2014 due to the fact that pretty much all binary options brokers offered the same kind of services and some decided to offer something new for a change.

Long term binary options are essentially options that have unusually long expiration times. What I mean here are expiration times of at least one day ranging to up to several weeks and months.

Usually these options are not that much advertised by the brokers and there is a specific reason for this. This is because long-term options have the best winning odds among all the possible binary options and strategies of binary options with long expiration times are the easiest to implement.

On this page, I will tell you exactly why long-term binary options are the easiest to win and how you can use them to your advantage.

Edit: I remember back in 2013 when I first started writing about binary options I pretty much wrote it everywhere that unless brokers would start to offer long-term options binary options would resemble more to gambling than real trading.

Now that we finally do have long-term options, I officially declare binary options a form of real trading. ☺

As explained above, long-term binary options contracts are options that have expiration times of at least one full day up to several weeks or even months.

Traditionally, binary options expiration times ranged from 30 seconds to a maximum of one or two hours. For the past few years, these were the only expiration times available at pretty much every binary options broker.

There were two main reasons why brokers began to introduce long-term binary options at around 2014. First, every broker pretty much offered the same services and therefore some decided to offer long-term options in order to differentiate themselves from others.

Second, binary options managed around 2014 to attract mainstream attention and the review and critique of real investors and old-school Forex traders. These people have pointed out that short-term options offer a hard time for newbies to make money, as these options are very hard to predict.

These expert traders (rightfully) claimed that binary options could only become a real form of investing and trading if brokers would stop restricting the maximum expiration times of options.

It was pointed out that real investing is a long-term process, meaning that traders should be given the opportunity to trade long-term binary options if binary options are to be regarded a proper form of trading and not just a funny game of chance and luck.

How Long Term Binary Options Strategy Works?

There is a very specific reason why these kind of options are much easier to predict that short-term options. It's because the longer an expiration time is, the less volatile the markets are overall and the better your judgment can be in making a prediction.

If you take longer times frames, you can also account for major events that are expected to happen during that time frame that might influence the movement of an asset. You cannot do this with short time frames.

Imagine the following:

You know that Apple will launch a new iPhone in 2 weeks. Based on this information how do you think the stock prices of Apple will move right after the iPhone launch? Will they decline or will they increase? – Obviously, they will increase most of the time in such a situation. This is what happens most of the time after a launch.

And that's it. Using a long-term binary options strategy you just made money in binary options. The reason why you made money was because you accounted for an expected major event that resulted in your asset's price increasing.

This strategy is impossible to implement using short-term options only. It is not possible to use a major news event to predict the movement of an asset during just a few seconds or minutes.

So, in other words, long-term binary options strategies involve accounting in for major news events that are expected to influence the value of an asset. I personally claim that this is the easiest way to make money in binary options.

Chapter 7: Short Term Vs Long Term Binary Strategy

As I have explained above it is not possible to account for the effect of news events when it comes to short-term options (30 seconds, 5 minutes etc.); in these cases the only strategy you can use is that of technical analysis.

Technical analysis is an advanced form of strategy that involves you having to read and interpret various charts and use different indicators. This is very difficult for most people because reading charts and such is a bit complicated if you don't already have a solid fundamental of financial trading.

On the other hand, when it comes to long-term binary strategies all you need to know is when a major event (such as new product launch) is taking place and then make the appropriate investment.

Real and to-the-point examples of long-term options strategies

Below you will find actual examples of the application of this strategy. You can do exactly what's described in these examples and make money in binary options.

Example 1.

Apple is expected to launch a new iPhone in September 15 2016. You will wait around 2 weeks before this event and will buy a binary options contract that will expire on September 16th and predict that the value of Apple will be higher at that point that it is now.

And that's it; you just won in binary options. Sure, this is not 100% safe but historically speaking Apple's stocks usually increase after a new product launch.

Now, such an Apple event usually only happens 2 times per year. Surely, you need much more than 2 winning opportunities to make real money in binary options. But the thing is you can use this with any company such as: Microsoft, Google, Amazon (their Kindle products), Samsung, Sony, HP, etc.

You can literally find out within 10 minutes of Google search when these companies have their annual events and product launches.

Example 2.

Microsoft is expected to give its annual revenue report on August 10 2016. Two weeks before the event you will do a quick Google search and check for industry predictions whether Microsoft made more money during the previous year or quarter.

If everyone expects the company to have made more money, you buy a long-term binary option predicting that Microsoft's stock prices will be go up on August 11th. If everyone seems to agree that the company made less money or that it stagnated, then you will buy a contract that predicts that Microsoft's value will decrease by August 11th.

The best thing about this strategy is that you can do this on much more occasions than just with the one on example 1.). There are hundreds of companies out there that might not even be as famous as Apple and Microsoft and might not 38even offer any products (they do services). You just need to Google their revenue report release dates and then Google what experts predict and then buy the appropriate binary options long-term contract.

And these are just two ways of making money in binary options with long-term strategies.

As you can see by now, this is perhaps the easiest way to make money. This is also the reason why brokers introduced this concept so late. The majority of traders don't even know these things and stick trading with short-term options. Now that you know all these, make sure to use them and you will likely make money in binary options.

Time Frame vs. Payouts

Binary options have many different types of payout profiles. Generally call and put binary options offer a payout between 70 and 85% for standard higher or lower binary options. These are options that allow an investor to receive a payout if the price of the underlying security is higher or lower from the market price of the security when the transaction takes place. Usually, brokers provide a lower payout as the expiration period declines. For example, a broker will generally offer a payout of 65-70% for short term options that are less than 120 seconds. Generally the payout increase as the expiration time of the option increases. Usually daily and weekly binary options have similar payout profiles that are at the high end of the spectrum.

One reason short term options have a lower payout is that many believe short term options are easier to speculate on when compared to longer term binary options. If you think about speculation as a 50-50 event, the question that needs to be asked is what's easier to speculate on, what'll happen in 24 hours from now, or what'll happen in the next minute?

For example, suppose it just started to rain outside, what's easier and more accurate to predict whether it will continue to rain for the next minute or the next 24 hours? With a 50-50 event, the shorter the timeframe you're trying to speculate on, the more accurate and profitable you can be.

Ability to Analyze a Market

Investors who are looking to trade binary options as a part time opportunity where they are looking at financial markets once a day when they come home from work should stick to longer term binary options. The amount of time you have to devote to the markets is a key factor in determining which time frame you should use. Traders who can devote hours to trading should look at longer term charts such as daily and weekly graphs, and in turn trade daily or weekly binary options. An investor who has a limited window of time to devote to analyzing charts or strategies should stick to evaluating long term or daily charts. Longer term charts paint a broader picture and it becomes easier to evaluate when compared to looking at many data points on a short term chart. Longer term charts will also allow a trader to look at many assets compared to short term charts.

Traders that spends most of the time analyzing price action and can devote time to watching intra-day market movements as well as economic and fundamental events can spend some of their time trading short term options and taking advantage of short term trends that takes place intra-day.

Short And Long Term Binary Options Strategies

As you gain more experience with trading binary options, you'll realize there are many binary options strategies to choose from. Selecting one largely depends on which asset you will be trading on as well as the expiration time. As you become more advanced in your approach, you can start to use some of the short and long-term strategies to help you improve your results.

In binary trading, there are three main expiration times – hourly, daily and weekly. Hourly options are short-term expiration times where a binary call or put option expires at the end of that particular hour either on the hour or on the half-hour. Daily options, also considered a short-term timeframe, expire at the end of the trading day. A long-term expiration time is that of a weekly option where the option expires at the end of the trading week.

For each type of expiration time, there is a binary trading strategy that's most appropriate.

Strategies for Hourly Options – Hedging & Risk Reversal Strategies

When trading hourly options, you need to implement strategies that take into account a short expiration time. Here are a couple of short-term strategies that are best suited when trading hourly options:

Hedging (or pairing) strategy – using a hedging strategy enables a trader to execute two options closely together in order to maximize his profits with a lower level of risk. For instance, if you successfully traded a call option on JPMorgan Chase & Co but believe it will fall in the next hour; you can implement a hedging strategy by pairing a put option on JPMorgan Chase & Co stock alongside a call option on the asset. This will allow you to hedge against both eventualities and safeguard your initial return.

Risk reversal strategy – using this strategy can be effective when trading on hourly options. If an asset is trending in a particular direction that isn't typical for the asset, you can place a trade on the asset which highlights that it is likely change course in a short space of time.

Strategies for Daily Options – Straddle & Knock-on Effect Strategies

Some of the binary options strategies that are most suitable for trading daily options are:

Straddle strategy – similar to the hedging strategy, the straddle strategy is more appropriate for daily options as it gives the asset a slightly longer timeframe to react to changes in the market. With this strategy, you would also place a call and a put option on an asset. However, you will also need to watch the movements of the asset very closely in order to ensure you know when to place the call or put option on the asset during the day.

Knock-on-effect strategy – the premise behind the knock-on effect strategy is that the movement of one option will have an effect on another. It is a useful strategy for traders who are trading daily options as it gives the subsequent asset time to react to the movements of the former. For instance, say Apple releases positive earnings for its 2nd quarter and its stock rises. In this instance, you could implement a knock-on effect strategy if you identify that the NASDAQ typically moves in line with Apple stock. A daily option would be ideal in this situation as it would give the index an opportunity to react to the changes experienced in Apple's stock.

Strategies for Weekly Options – Index-Asset Divergence & Commodity-Stock Affect Strategies

When trading weekly options, you need to implement strategies that take into account a long expiration time. Here are a couple of long-term strategies that are best suited when trading weekly options:

Index-asset divergence – when you are trading weekly options, one way to maximize your success is to understand the interrelationships between assets. If you choose this index-specific strategy, you would understand the immediate and long-term effects of a stock on the value of an index. If you notice that there is a pattern of both assets moving in the same direction but then a change at a later stage, this is the strategy for you. To use this strategy, you would first execute a weekly options trade on a company's stock and then execute an opposite trade on an index the company is a component of.

Commodity stock affect – with this strategy, you'll try to use your knowledge of commodities and stocks to execute weekly options trades. Since the value of commodities fluctuates, market analysts are typically looking at upward or downwards trends to speculate on future movements. This commentary then influences other assets, such as stocks. For instance, if analysts are suggesting that the value of oil is rising, this will create an effect on stocks in the oil and gas industry, as well as in manufacturing sectors.

In addition to hourly, daily and weekly options, many of you may have heard about 60-second binary options. These options have an expiration time of 60 seconds, where traders find out whether their trade was successful or not in just one minute. Although it is great to experience a potential profit in such a quick timeframe, it is challenging to experience consistent returns in only 60 seconds. Assets fluctuate on a minute-to-minute basis but they tend to exhibit general trends over an hour, day or week. A minute turnaround can force you to engage in a guessing game – much like gambling – while the main benefit of binary options trading is that you can develop a defined strategy to grow your profitability

Whether you're looking to execute trades using hourly, daily or weekly options, there are short and long-term strategies that can help you succeed. As you continue to refine your binary trading strategy, applying a strategy that's best suited for your particular trade will surely help you achieve your greatest potential.

Conclusion

Thank you again for buying this book!

I hope this book was able to help you to feel more knowledgeable about the world of binary options.

If you are interested, the next step is to continue researching the subject. While some believe that stocks only work for some and not for others, or require a certain type of intelligence, this is not true, and anyone with a willingness to learn can get into this field. I hope that you found this book interesting and are ready to take the next step on your journey into penny stocks. Although this book is a great starting point, it's far from all you need. You have only just delved into the vast world that is Binary options with this book.

Thank you and good luck!

17205812R00031

Printed in Poland
by Amazon Fulfillment
Poland Sp. z o.o., Wrocław